Tarot Reading Explained

The Ultimate Tarot Guide for Beginners

Tarot Overview, Basics of Tarot Reading, Major and Minor Arcana, Interpretations, History, Reading Techniques, and More!

By Riley Star

Copyrights and Trademarks

Disclaimer and Legal Notice

Foreword

Tarot reading is a method for further exploring the unknown places in one's subconscious mind. It's not an exact science and this kind of system will not foretell one's future but rather give a person an idea of how one should act in relation to the messages being portrayed or sent out by the cards. It can provide a glimpse of the past, suggests how to handle the present and become a guide for the future.

This book will provide you with a wealth of information about tarot and tarot reading; the basics of each cards, elements and suits, its significance, its history, the different interpretations, the possible connections and the types of reading as well as the memorization techniques.

Table of Contents

Chapter One: The Art of Tarot

So let's get right into it! "How can a deck of cards tell a person anything about anything?" This is the common question that people asks for many years since the 'art of tarot' was invented. And while there's no exact or proven based answer to this question, it makes you wonder why despite of that, there are still a lot of people who are willing to study this field, become experts at it, and even make a living out of it. Why there are still people out there who are willing to draw out cards, believe in what the tarot readers tell them, and believe in the power of the colorful yet sometimes disturbing imagery depicted on the cards and relate it somehow to every area of their lives? I mean it's just a photo of something – and it's just a piece of card! How can it possibly tell you anything? The weird part is that more often than not these cards somehow do tell what a person is currently going through and sometimes it also shows a glimpse of the future. How does that happen?

Perhaps, the question is not how, but why. And the funny thing about the 'why' question is that it's one of life's biggest mystery. That even if you get to the bottom of it, there's no answer that will satisfy your curiosity or there's no answer that will make sense. Sometimes you just have to trust in something and not question how it happens. It just is. It's like life – it just happens.

For me, this is how everyone should approach tarot; you have every right to question the methods, the meanings, the cards, the readers, the 'energies' or whatnot but at the end of the day it's what you believe in, it's your personal 'why,' it's about your intuition – you don't exactly know but you just do. This is why tarot in itself is an art. It's a free form, sure there are some guidelines and rules on how one should interpret or read it but there are no standards of what is right or wrong, of what is positive or negative. It's not black and white. It's not absolute. It's about belief, intuition, trust and perhaps it's all about having faith - faith in what the cards are possibly telling you, faith in the tarot reader that will send you the message, and faith in yourself that will ultimately decide your life's fate.

History and Origin of Tarot

Tarot's origin is also a mystery in itself because there are no proofs of where it originally came from, how it was invented and for what purpose. Many historians believed that it came from Italy around the 15th century and were only used as a simple cards game. Wealthy people who patronize the game commissioned artful decks that some of which have survived to this day. One example of an early version is the Visconti – Sforza deck which was created around 1450.

Around the 18th century, it was believed that scholars discovered the tarot decks and became fascinated by the cards' imagery. These people realized that the images depicted on the card could mean something 'powerful' and it's not an ordinary deck. These scholars possibly created the art of the tarot card reading because they're the ones who connected the cards to various fields including Hermetic philosophy, alchemy, Egyptian mysteries, the Kabbalah and other mystical systems. The tarot card reading became more than just a game during the turn of the 20th century, at one point it even became a practice in secret societies one of which is the Order of the Golden Dawn. As time goes by, tarot eventually became known worldwide and many types of decks as well as layouts were created and developed.

Tarot cards today are used as a tool to connect to oneself, the world and the divine. The art of tarot reading has three elements – the seekers, the readers and the tarot cards. Once it is shuffled and drawn, the chosen cards will be laid out in a pattern called the spread wherein the positions have meaning as well. The tarot reader will then combine both the card's meaning and the patterns to hopefully shed light or give some answers to the seeker's queries.

We may never know the true origin of the tarot cards, how the scholars drew meaning from it or how people over the years have developed a system for reading but just like any other types of techniques developed that concerns our unconscious minds such as meditation, psychotherapy, and visualizations, tarot is just another tool to explore one's mindset.

Chapter Two: Basic Meanings of Tarot Cards

In this chapter, you'll learn the basic meanings of the tarot cards. You don't really need to memorize every meaning or interpretation of each card right away but you have to at least know its background or the values, ideas and principles it represents so that you can understand how it could relate to another card or to an aspect of one's life. You'll also get to learn the general meaning of the 'types' of cards found in the deck – they are called the Major Arcana and the Minor Arcana as well as what each suits (Wands, Swords, Pentacles and Cups) represent.

You may notice that some cards have almost the same meaning or is somewhat related to one another, but as you learn more in the next chapters, you'll soon find out how the message of each card within each suit and its positions could tell a different story or may be interpreted from a different perspective.

The Major and Minor Arcana

The tarot deck is made up of 78 cards that are divided into two sections – the major arcana and the minor. Arcana or Arcanum means "profound secrets" according to the alchemists from the Middle Ages. They believe that the tarot cards are a collection of these 'secrets' that explains the nature, life, unconscious mind and the universe.

The Major Arcana consist of 22 cards and they are considered as the "heart of the deck." These cards also represent sort of the 'bigger picture' during reading. It mostly symbolizes some kind of inherent aspect of human experience or patterns that influences human nature. The major arcana is given utmost importance during a tarot reading since these cards represent a person's most basic concerns and often times involves the spiritual aspect and inner self. It starts from the card of beginnings called The Fool (0) and ends in a card called The World (22).

The numbers also correspond and are correlated with the numbers of the cards in the minor arcana. The Minor Arcana is composed of 56 cards which are divided into four suits – the Wands, Cups, Swords and Pentacles. Each of the suits also has Court Cards (The Page, The Knight, The Queen and The King) and Pip Cards that are numbered from 1 to 10. The minor arcana deals with a more universal and practical theme, its concern about the emotions, struggles and events of the day to day life of an individual. In the next section, you'll see the meanings, words, and interpretations of each card in the major and minor arcana as well as the general meaning of each suits and court cards.

THE MAJOR ARCANA

THE FOOL (0)

- A new phase of life begins
- The discovery of talents
- New experiences
- A risk must be taken
- There's a need to abandon the old and start something
- Personal growth
- New development

THE MAGICIAN (1)

- Possibilities in a person
- New skills are available
- Potential is growing
- Opportunities and adventures unfolding
- Success in everything if a person utilizes his/her skills and talents

THE EMPRESS (2)

- Known as the mother of fertility and growth
- New things about to enter a situation
- There may be a birth coming or a new path in life
- Focuses on marriage, relationship, pregnancy, patience and motherhood

THE EMPEROR (3)

- A need to make something solid or to solidify something
- Focuses on building an idea or something with a firm structure
- Have values of authority, control and dominance.
- Man of power
- An employer or an authority

THE HIGH PRIESTESS (4)

- A time for reflection
- Allows secrets to be revealed
- Shows potential abundance
- Urges people to pay attention to your dreams and intuition
- This card is all about truly understanding life's possibilities

THE HIEROPHANT (5)

- There's a need for spiritual purpose
- Talks about the search for a personal philosophy
- Encourages a person to increase studying and learning
- Focuses on humility and teachings
- Makes a person get through deeply frightening and hard situations
- This card can sometimes suggest marriage or a serious turn towards religion

THE LOVERS (6)

- A love affair with a trial or choice attached
- This card indicates that these decisions or choices are incredibly important and significant

- One must choose the right path
- A sign of true partnership
- It focuses in choosing intuitively rather than by the use of intellect

THE CHARIOT (7)

- Conflict within
- Struggles and battles
- Potential for victory
- Resolution of fights
- Moving forward
- Overcoming opposition through confidence
- Control and Determination
- It can also mean a journey or change of location

JUSTICE (8)

- Need for clarity of mind
- Impartial judgment
- Requires a balanced intellect
- Legal matters needing attention
- Calls for the fairest decision
- A person is also being called to account for one's actions and will be judged accordingly

THE TEMPERANCE (9)

- Harmony within relationships
- Suggests happy marriage or partnership
- Adaptation and coordination
- Balance
- Patience
- Moderation

THE STRENGTH (10)

- Suggests a person must face the things or the truth in a situation that you have been putting off for too long.
- Overcoming one's fears or doubts
- Courage
- Inner Will
- Optimism

THE HERMIT (11)

- A time for withdrawal
- Promotes silent meditation and solitude
- Patience is needed to confront one's inner world
- Could be someone who likes to or needs to work alone

THE WHEEL OF FORTUNE (12)

- Change in fortune
- New beginnings
- Suggests new chapter in life
- The Wheel makes a new turn
- Remain optimistic
- Someone who have faith that the Universe will take care of the situation

THE HANGED MAN (13)

- Sacrifice must be made to gain something of greater value
- Talks about waiting in order to allow new possibilities to arise
- Vulnerability
- Selflessness
- New Perspectives
- Suggests a willingness to adapt in changing circumstances

DEATH (14)

- Known as the most misunderstood card in the deck
- The end of something which has been lived out

- Suggests transformation or new beginnings will follow
- This card indicates a time of significant change and transition

THE DEVIL (15)

- A confrontation with the inner world
- Facing fears and inhibitions can foster growth
- The Devil reflects actual addictions and dependencies in one's life like alcohol, illegal drugs, toxic relationships, gambling, overspending
- Also suggest breaking of bad or unhealthy habits or vices

THE TOWER (16)

- Focuses on breaking down existing forms
- Changing false structures and finding true values
- Change around the home
- Emotionally challenging periods in a person's life
- A time of great upheaval
- It symbolizes conflict and overall disruption but it's for the greater good

THE STAR (17)

- It's about facing things you have been reluctant to deal with
- It could lead to good or bad things but this action needs to done

THE MOON (18)

- Fluctuation
- Uncertainty
- Confusion
- Passive
- Suggests of letting go of one's conscious mental blocks
- Encourages a person to allow his/her intuition to guide him/her

THE SUN (19)

- Optimism
- Passive
- Energetic or Vitality
- Abundance
- A time of clear vision
- It is about embracing your destiny and giving it everything you have got.
- Suggests happiness , triumph and good health

- Also relates to achievement
- Sometimes talks about traveling to a warm or tropical climate

JUDGEMENT (20)

- It's a time for reaping rewards for past actions and reaching conclusions
- Suggests that a person may have assessed and evaluated his/her past experiences and have learned from them
- Rebirth or renewal
- Changes for the better
- Getting well after a long sickness
- Also suggests finding a new career or spiritual path

THE WORLD (21)

- Success
- Achievement
- Attainment
- The realization of a goal or the completion of a cycle
- Can also indicate world travel
- Suggests a feeling of being welcome anywhere you go

THE MINOR ARCANA

WANDS SUIT– wands is related to one's imagination and creativity, it is associated with the element of fire. It also focuses on action and movement and has risk – taking qualities to it as well as confidence, inward passion and enthusiasm.

Court Cards:

PAGE OF WANDS

- Serves as the instigator
- Curious and restless
- Suggests a creative Spark

KNIGHT OF WANDS

- Adventurer
- Has a youthful enthusiasm
- Has appetite for risks
- Someone who is in search for challenge and excitement

QUEEN OF WANDS

- Usually motivated and dynamic

- Someone who knows how to multi – task
- She's a heroine and charming but can also be selfish at times

KING OF WANDS

- Has a forceful personality
- Visionary
- Willful
- Reckless
- Extremely creative and inventive
- Sometimes it can also mean that he's not paying attention to details

Pip Cards:

ACE OF WANDS (1)

- Has a lot of creative energy, drive and vitality
- Has potential for success
- Initiative
- Boundless Energy
- Creative Power and Inspiration

TWO OF WANDS

- Suggests a more intuitive choice

- Two possibilities or duality
- Suggests equally good
- Firm plans should be done
- Envisioning the future
- Readiness for change
- Suggests that a person is standing in his past and future

THREE OF WANDS

- Suggests a stage of initial completion of a creative project
- Ideas are forming
- There are forces of new energy that is being generated
- Readiness to embark on a new adventure
- Taking opportunities
- Can also be about travelling

FOUR OF WANDS

- A time to pause for celebration after hard efforts
- Also suggests that a person should take a break, have a period of rest and learn to relax
- Sometimes it's known as the marriage card
- Harmony in one's home
- Aesthetic pleasures
- Positive connections

FIVE OF WANDS

- A time of struggle
- Challenges will constantly appear
- Expect difficulties ahead
- Open conflict
- Certain issues cause a lot of tension and confusion
- Lacking focus
- Suggests inner conflict or general chaos
- Can also mean that an individual is being pulled in different directions

SIX OF WANDS

- Public recognition
- Promotion
- Recognition for one's work
- Suggest success in any chosen field
- Supportive community

SEVEN OF WANDS

- Stiff competition must now be faced
- A person should holds one's ground
- Renewed determination
- Courage is necessary
- Suggests inner or outer battles

- It can also mean that an individual is prepared for a fight

EIGHT OF WANDS

- It's a card of ease, everything is happening in a fast pace
- There's a real sense of harmony
- Swiftness
- It's a period of fruitful progress after a delay or struggle
- Suggests that everything is in a person's favor but needs to continue pushing forward

NINE OF WANDS

- Strength in reserve can provide enough energy to win the battle
- The energy of a person seems exhausted but it suggests that one should still move forward to reach completion
- Requires perseverance
- Acknowledges weariness before a resolution can occur

TEN OF WANDS

- There could be a danger implied in taking on more than one can cope with
- Inadequate awareness of one's limitations
- Can also mean that the passion can be renewed since a new cycle is coming
- It means a release from struggle

CUPS SUIT – The cups card is the suit that is related to the element of water. It relates to the inner realm not just pertaining to a person's emotions but also one's unconscious mind, dreams and intuition. It can also relate to relationships but in a deeper way.

Court Cards:

PAGE OF CUPS

- Vulnerable
- Introspection
- Emotional Sensitivity

KNIGHT OF CUPS

- Dreamer
- Soft spoken
- Easy going and gentle

- Sincere

QUEEN OF CUPS

- Emotionally intense
- Can be intuitive and determined
- Can also be jealous and ruthless

KING OF CUPS

- Has a strong and controlling force
- Resists change in an emotional status quo
- One who likes to maintain power especially in relationships

Pip Cards:

ACE OF CUPS (1)

- High feelings and emotion
- New relationships
- Love affair
- The birth of a child
- Self – acceptance
- Spiritual guidance
- Gratitude and compassion

TWO OF CUPS

- Commitment to romance
- Partnership or friendship
- Emotional balance
- There's an attraction of two things or people even if it comes from different natures

THREE OF CUPS

- Suggest a celebration
- A time for rejoicing
- The commitment to a future project or endeavor has been made
- Suggests social life and successful partnerships/groups even from different natures
- Compatibility

FOUR OF CUPS

- Usually the person is self-absorbed
- An individual is content with the way things are
- Stability and confinement in terms of emotion
- There's an emotional uncertainty or self – doubt
- Someone who is not sure if they want to make a change
- Inability to make decisions
- Emotionally stuck

FIVE OF CUPS

- Regret over past actions
- Loss or betrayal in love
- Separation
- All is not lost even though it suggests loss
- Suggests that one should recognize what has been lost

SIX OF CUPS

- Past effort may bring present rewards
- Can also mean that an old lover may appear again
- Sentimental time
- Also known as a sibling card
- Mutual enjoyment in partnership

SEVEN OF CUPS

- Focuses on several choice available
- Careful decisions must be made
- Action
- There is a risk of illusion
- You need to avoid escapism protect yourself against unclear thinking
- Also suggests search for wisdom or oneself
- Emotional confusion

- Self – doubt and can also be about projection of problems into the outer world and how one should take responsibility for it

EIGHT OF CUPS

- Can mean that a person must leave the past behind
- Letting go of something even if it required much effort
- Suggests of walking away
- Encourages a person to pursue one's dream or ambitions
- Change of relationship status
- Emotional detachment
- Has willingness to walk into the unknown

NINE OF CUPS

- A wish of paramount importance will come true
- Feelings of tremendous joy
- An emotional journey is almost over or will come to fruition
- Contentment

TEN OF CUPS

- Happiness and contentment

- A sense of permanence and future purpose
- It often suggests starting a family
- The sense of harmony
- Also suggests marriage
- Can also indicate responsibilities within a community

SWORDS SUIT– deals with how a person speak, how one perceives the world, an individual's belief system, how one makes decisions and understand things. The suit of Swords has the most problematic points in the tarot deck but it is the nature of air and the mind.

Court Cards:

PAGE OF SWORDS

- Has a quality of wit and carelessness
- Also suggests immature thoughts

KNIGHT OF SWORDS

- Communicator
- Someone who loves to learn and interested in new ideas
- Very expressive or talkative

QUEEN OF SWORDS

- Advocate
- Someone who has high principles
- Doesn't compromise or negotiate
- Someone who is emotional and critical

KING OF SWORDS

- Enforcer
- Someone who upholds the laws or values
- One who leads and decides
- Sometimes unsympathetic

Pip Cards

ACE OF SWORDS (1)

- Inevitable and irrevocable change
- Awakening of mental powers
- Conflict can somehow arise at the start but are ultimately beneficial to the growth of the person
- Also called the sword of polarity or the sword of absolute knowledge
- It's a card of mind empowerment

TWO OF SWORDS

- Stalemate; ambiguity
- Nothing can move or change
- Suggests great tension or deep hostility
- A person must make choices
- Having an inner focus in oneself
- Can also be about denial

THREE OF SWORDS

- Quarrels and conflict
- A period of challenges or flux for relationships
- It also suggests that something sad or painful must be allowed to work something out
- Heartbreak or pain
- Disappointment; delusions
- Also suggest healing and assessment of situation

FOUR OF SWORDS

- A need for rest or retreat after stress
- A time for reconciliation after tension
- Recuperation
- Suggests peace despite turmoil
- Postponement of decisions

FIVE OF SWORDS

- Also known as the boundary card
- Indicates contradiction
- Pride must be swallowed
- Limitations must be recognized before further progress can be made
- Suggests that a person must work within the framework of that situation

SIX OF SWORDS

- A card of harmony
- A period of calm after great anxiety
- Release of tension
- A peaceful journey towards smoother waters
- Also suggest that a person should physically move away from unpleasant environment
- Indicates physical travel or postponement of decision because the mind is inactive

SEVEN OF SWORDS

- A need for evasion and avoidance of direct confrontation in order to achieve a goal
- One must be use his/her logical thinking, tact, and diplomacy instead of aggression
- Avoidance of conflict

- Sometimes known as the card of deceit or secrets
- Sometimes not wanting to face something or someone who hides the truth

EIGHT OF SWORDS

- A fear of moving out of a situation in relationships
- Can also suggests a situation of tension but in this case, the choices are perfectly conscious
- It also talks about how one's perceptions block the will
- There could be fear of change
- The belief system could get a person stuck which is why the card suggests that an individual must think of something or perceive something in a different way

NINE OF SWORDS

- A time in which the mind is experiencing fears due to bad thought
- Nightmares and fantasies trouble the mind of the individual
- Can also mean that the end of mental struggle is near
- Anxiety and being overwhelmed
- There's a sense of worry and doom

TEN OF SWORDS

- The end of a painful situation or state
- There emerges an ability to see a situation practicality
- A fresh start is expected
- The start of the new cycle is about to begin which brings new hope
- A new horizon is near despite of the previous struggles

PENTACLES SUIT – the suit of pentacles is not just about money or financial matters, it's also about tangible or material things. It's also about the practical and pragmatic side, the stability and security in the physical world. It's also about how one's belief system, spirituality and creative tendencies play out in one's life.

Court Cards:

PAGE OF PENTACLES

- Apprentice
- Someone who has a plan and undertakes a long term activity
- Indicates new beginnings and new perspective
- Someone who is earnest and grounded

KNIGHT OF PENTACLES

- Worker
- Someone who is reliable and more mechanical
- Resourceful
- Doesn't move fast and takes his time in doing something
- Someone who exert steady effort to achieve something

QUEEN OF PENTACLES

- Nurturer
- Represents constancy and comfort
- Someone who is self – employed and one who takes charge of their own life
- Calm but not complacent
- Industrious

KING OF PENTACLES

- Entrepreneur
- Somebody who knows how to make money and provides security
- Someone who knows how to build things that will last

Pip Cards:

ACE OF PENTACLES (1)

- Material achievement is possible
- Financial aid may be available for the beginning of a new venture
- New opportunities that is related to work or home
- New growth in every aspect of one's life (home, health, career)

TWO OF PENTACLES

- Change and fluctuation in financial matters
- There'll be optimism and enthusiasm which balances out the anxieties when it comes to financial matters
- Transition
- There could be some sort of instability but not chaotic
- Flexible and can have many options, the key is to being open

THREE OF PENTACLES

- A satisfactory period for a person
- Initial completion of work
- A basic structure is built which still requires further development
- Can indicate effective partnerships or collaboration
- Has a firm foundation

FOUR OF PENTACLES

- There is danger in clinging too tightly to whatever a person has gained or accumulated
- Nothing is lost, but nothing can be gained either
- Resistance to change
- Focuses on self – preservation or maintaining one's position

FIVE OF PENTACLES

- Financial loss and hardship
- Loss of luck especially in health
- Loss on a deeper level of self - confidence
- Loss of faith in oneself or life
- Expectation of failure
- Deprivation mentality
- Can indicate lack of spiritual connection

SIX OF PENTACLES

- Help from a generous friend or employer
- Suggest a situation in which there is money or good fortune to be shared among people
- Shared resources
- Mutually beneficial

SEVEN OF PENTACLES

- A difficult decision must be made between material security and uncertain new opportunities
- Focuses about patience and taking time to make things happen
- There's availability of options
- Suggests reevaluation and can also indicate lack of motivation

EIGHT OF PENTACLES

- The apprentice, training or starting out a new endeavor in another profession
- Re- arrangement or re- alignment of priorities in any aspect
- One should take a new focus

NINE OF PENTACLES

- A card of great satisfaction and pleasure
- There'll be a reward for effort or material benefits
- Confidence in one's abilities
- Someone who celebrates life
- Appreciation for the good thing that is happening in one's life
- Someone who is self - reliant

TEN OF PENTACLES

- Financial stability and foundation for home and family
- A new phase in life is about to come
- Denotes values of society, cultural traditions, morals and marriage (something that is unlikely to change or something that is secure)

Court Cards

There are 16 personality cards or commonly known in tarot as the court cards. Court cards have these following characteristics that you need to keep in mind:

- **Court Cards stay true to their element**

  They live, breathe and die in the nature of the suit that they represent. Say for example if a court card shows up and it belongs to the suit of pentacles, you can expect that this card cares about practicality, it's grounded and deals with the concrete side of any issue since pentacles are of earth elements. The court card belonging to the wands suit represents challenges, creativity and the self – expressive quality.

- **Court Cards are not gender or age specific**

  Court cards express energies but it doesn't pertain to a certain age or gender. Say for example, you pulled the Queen of Cups it doesn't necessarily mean that it's about a woman; it could mean that it's about somebody who has characteristics, reactions or experiences related to what the Queen of Cups card is denoting. It can be quite tricky sometimes to not look at the gender or age that is being depicted in the card.

- **Court Cards reflects level of experience with a certain element**

  The Pages card within each suit are the least mature, the Knights are more adventurous, the Queens serve as the channel or vehicles in which the element can be fully expressed, and the Kings are the leaders or masters because it has characteristics that likes to have control over the element and sometimes are personally creative with the element. You have to keep in mind though, that there's no such thing as a good card or a bad card, there's no absolute positive or negative card, there could be a positive or negative approach depending on the situation but there's no card on the deck that is intrinsically good or bad.

- **Court Cards work best if the question is properly phrased**

  How you phrase the subject's query or question will give you as a reader a format or context in which the question will be answered. Court cards can mean different things, so instead of just randomly pulling out a card, it's best to have a proper context or determine a certain aspect.

Chapter Three: Types of Tarot Layouts/Spread

In this chapter, you'll learn the most common tarot spreads or layouts for beginners and also for expert tarot readers. Be reminded though that this is listed in no particular order. You'll also get to learn the meaning of each spread so you can easily connect the cards and be able to answer your client's question more accurately. It's up to you to determine which spread might work best for any type of reading, it's probably best to learn them all so you can have the chance to see what's more appropriate for you and your subjects. Now, let's lay down the cards on the table!

Most Common Tarot Layouts or Spreads

The True Love Layout

This spread or layout focuses on a person's relationship, but not just about one's romantic relationship (although it's the most common topic among seekers). It's also use to evaluate a person's physical, spiritual and emotional connection to their current or potential partners. It's a six card spread and the pattern signifies a certain interpretation.

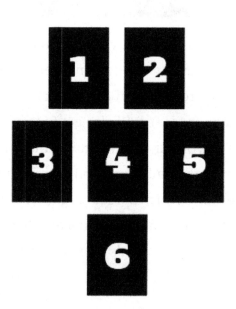

#1 Card: Signifies how the seeker feels about the current relationship that he/she is in. It also includes one's outlook towards the relationship.

#2 Card: Signifies the seeker's partner (either spouse, boyfriend/girlfriend) and his/her feelings about the relationship as well as one's expectations

#3 Card: Represents the connection or common characteristics of the seeker and his/her partner

#4 Card: Represents the qualities of strength in the relationship

#5 Card: Represents the weakness qualities of the relationship and the things both parties should improve on

#6: Represents how the relationship is going to go or what needs to be done to maintain or perhaps create a more meaningful connection with one another.

The Success Layout

Obviously this type of spread is concern about an individual's successes in terms of career, dreams or even in oneself. This kind of layout will also help a person in how to overcome certain challenges and could also get some advice on how to achieve a resolution to a problem. It may also represent the things an individual already has like the resources or skills that are available. It's also a five – card spread with this layout:

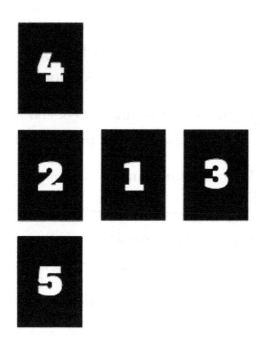

#1 Card: Represents the main challenge or problem of the seeker

#2 Card: Represents the complications from those challenges

#3 Card: Denotes some factors that the seeker needs to know which are affecting the current situation

#4 Card: Signifies the people or ideas that could make the seeker grow to achieve a certain goal

#5 Card: Indicates what the seeker needs to do to achieve a goal, avoid failure as much as possible and become successful in an endeavor.

The Celtic - Cross Layout

The Celtic – Cross spread is one of the most complex types of tarot reading but it's perhaps one of the most original layouts and it has been used for many centuries. The layout's versatility has been helpful in assessing complicated queries because it can be read in different ways depending on the card's combinations and patterns. This kind of layout basically focuses on the seeker's issues as well as the outside factors that are at play. This type of layout may be quite hard to understand especially for beginners but of course practice can make you better. This is a 10 – card spread with this layout:

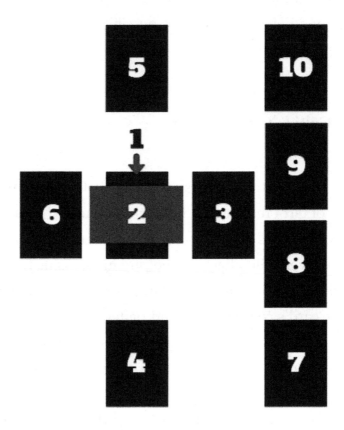

#1 Card: Represents the seeker's current situation

#2 Card: It represents what's holding a person back or what is helping him/her

#3 Card: Focuses more on the seeker's true desire that he/she may be unaware of, as well as the subconscious influences that ultimately affects his/her life

#4 Card: Represents the past events and issues that are still bothering the seeker

#5 Card: Focuses on one's conscious desires and the goals that are very important for the seeker. It can also tell where the person should place his/her energy and how one should use that energy to accomplish an objective.

#6 Card: Represents one's path – either positive or negative. If it's particularly negative, the card in this placement can also tell the seeker how he/she can avoid it or bounce back from it.

#7 Card: Represents the seeker's attitude, ideals and actions

#8 Card: Represents the kind of energy that the seeker gets from the people surrounding him/her and if this energy is helpful or not

#9 Card: Also known as the revelation card; it denotes that there are things that should not be neglected and one must pay attention to such things because it can have a huge impact in the current or possible situations.

#10 Card: This is the final outcome of a situation and it is also related to the #5 card. It will tell the reader and the seeker if the energy in a particular issue is complementing or conflicting one another.

Chapter Four: Tips in Memorizing Your Deck

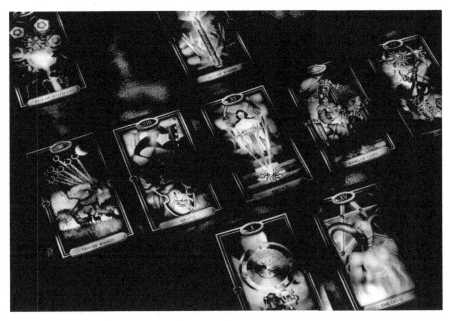

Before you memorize tarot cards, there are three important things that you need to keep in mind. These three tips will serve as the building blocks of understanding the meaning, impact and perhaps significance of each card in any kind of position, flow or question. You are also provided with three methods on how you can draw meaning from the cards or how you can easily interpret them. Be reminded that the methods given in this chapter are only basics and mostly targeted for beginners.

Tip #1: Learn Your Deck's Structure

Being familiar with your tarot deck will help you memorize your cards more including the impact or meanings of the cards belonging in the major and minor ones. The tarot deck is composed of 22 Major Arcana (0 – 21) and 56 Minor Arcana (16 Court Cards; 40 Pip Cards – compose of 10 for each 4 suits).If you want to learn the meanings of the cards, you have to separate them out and individually learn them in different kinds of situations or reading types, before you'll be able to connect them to one another, you have to know their individual significance.

The Major Arcana are cards focuses on the spiritual and psychological experiences of an individual. It also denotes the inner growth or development of a person. The Minor Arcana are composed of tarot cards that are relating to everyday life or relating to situations with people as well as how an individual is dealing with the daily life and the struggles that come along with it.

Tip #2: Be Familiar with the Four Suits

There are four suits in the minor arcana; these are pentacles (earth), swords (air), cups (water), wands (fire). It's important to understand the nature of these four suits and the meaning of the ten tarot cards within each suit.

Tip #3: Learn How to Interpret Numbers

The numbers for each suit is composed of 1 to 10; each number within each suit has a specific meaning that you need to understand. Sometimes numbers have a relatively similar meaning but the only difference is the aspect or how you look at it while also considering the suit that it came from. So if it's number ten for example, ten means the end of a cycle, if it's ten of cups it might pertain to the end of an emotional journey, if it's ten of swords it could mean the end of the struggles for that person etc. that's why it could be focusing on the different aspect of an individual but the number relatively has the same meaning.

Tip #4: Choose Cards that has a Common Imagery

This is particularly helpful for beginners, most expert readers recommend buying tarot cards that has common imagery to help you easily remember because there are some tarot decks that will look kind of unusual and sometimes hard to remember. So try to buy tarot cards that are friendly to you or speak to you because that way you can be easily familiar with it and you're not going to struggle to figure out what kind it is while you're doing the reading.

Tip #5: Use keywords for memorization

Now there are a lot of tarot cards and apart from memorizing its literal meaning, you also have to keep in mind its elements, the suits, the numbers and its significance or relation to one another etc., so there's a lot of things you need to remember and consider while doing a reading which is why keywords can help because it can make you associate or connect the meaning of a particular card and its significance since words are also connected with one another somehow. You can use at least 3 or 4 keywords for each card especially if you're just starting to learn this craft. It will take a period of time before you fully memorize and understand the meaning of each card so you have to really commit in studying this art if you want to become a proficient reader or be able to give an accurate reading.

Methods for Memorization

In this section, you'll learn some methods or ways on how you can memorize the meanings of each card.

Method 1: Connect Keywords

As mentioned earlier, you may want to use keywords for each card as well as the elements involve. So always remember three or four keywords for the numbers, for the elements, and for each suit and then combine these keywords to draw a meaning. For example, you pulled out a Three of Pentacles card, you can dissect it down by having a keyword for the number three, for the pentacles suit, for the element of pentacles which is earth, and then just combine those keywords so that it can form a meaning. Connecting your keywords with the number, element and suit is one of the ways in which you can start reading the tarot cards and relating it to an aspect in your subject's life.

Method 2: Draw Meanings from the Imagery/Symbols in the Card

If you don't like using keywords or you're the kind of person who possibly can derive much better meanings from pictures instead of memorizing words, you can use this method during your reading and then just relate the depicted imagery to one another. Of course you still have to know the basic meaning behind each object or symbol in the card but for some people they can easily remember those keywords if they literally describe the pictures and expound the meaning from there.

Method 3: Memorize meanings by associating it with people or circumstances

Another great method you can use that can be very effective in remembering the meaning of your tarot cards is if you associate it with people or circumstances. You can associate a card with something that has perhaps a personal meaning to you that whenever you think about it, you will remember. If it helps, you can also associate it with a story from your personal life that can be related to the meaning of the card so you can easily remember it.

Chapter Five: Numbers and the Major Arcana

In this chapter you'll learn the meaning of numbers as well as the pattern within a reading with regard to the numbers of the tarot card. As you may have noticed the cards in the major arcana also have corresponding numbers to it which makes them somewhat related or can be correlated with the meaning of the numbers in the pip cards. This could give a more in – depth interpretation and significance in the card's message.

Ace Cards – Number One

Ace cards represent a cycle, a starting point, new beginnings or an upcoming phase. It can also relate to the pure potential in a suit, it's also associated with initiation, dreams and inspiration. It's all about opportunity for growth as well. The ace card is also related to the Magician card in the Major Arcana.

- **Ace Cards and the Magician**
  The Magician card is the number one is the major arcana deck. Most magician cards have all the elements of each suit, you can see in the magician card imagery that it there's a cup, swords, pentacles and a wand, the magician therefore has all the energies that are required in order to manifest in the physical world. It's also symbolic because the magician has access to all the energies or elements. The Magician card is also known as the creator or someone who can manifest because he recognizes that he has the tools and skills to create something, if you relate it to your subject it could mean that he/she has the will or ability to make something happen. It's through the pure potential of the energies or aces that enable the magician to channel or manifest things in life which makes them have related meanings.

The Number Two Cards

Number Two in tarot relates to the unity of the number one that creates duality or polarity. This number suggests partnership, requires reconciliation and a drive to find harmony and balanced out conflict. It also suggests tension, crossroads, and decision – making, it also relates to the High Priestess card in the major arcana.

- **The Number Two and the High Priestess**
  The High Priestess card in the major arcana relates to number two tarot cards because it also talks about duality and represents the conscious and unconscious sides, dark and light as well as spirit and matter realms. It also relates to the feminine aspects of life like one's intuition, contemplation and suggests that one should take his/her time before making any decisions or doing something. The High Priestess is known as the holder of secrets as well. Number two cards don't just represent duality but also exhibits a level of balance. Both of these cards have a lot of similarities in terms of meaning as well as imagery, it's focusing on trusting one's intuition or inner feelings in making decisions to recognize what an individual need to do or the steps one needs to take next.

The Number Three Cards

Number Three in tarot represents creativity, growth, development as well as manifestation. It also represents friendship, groups or networking. Three also suggest that a creative project is on its initial stage and more development is needed. The number three also relates to the Empress card in the major arcana.

- **The Number Three and the Empress**
  The Empress card represents fertility, creativity and a nurturing nature. It also relates to the artistic side, and is known as the universal mother because it relates to the abundance of creation/ procreation. If you pulled out an Empress card and it is paired with a number three, it could pertain to a positive creation of a project; there could also be a sort of connection between people or having a fulfilling network. Basically when these cards are paired it talks about creativity, connection and abundance.

The Number Four Cards

Number four in tarot denotes stability, solid foundation, reliability, security, structure and stagnation. It can also relate to practicality or formation. The number four often times serve as the container for the energy of each suit, it forms an order but can have potential limitations or confinement. Four also relates to the Emperor in the major arcana.

- **The Number Four and the Emperor**
  The Emperor card is very much related to the number four because it talks about a leader, having a solid foundation and expressing firm decisions. It also exhibits an authoritative figure and even a father figure. Power and control are also involved when you pulled an emperor card with a four, it will focus more on leadership and the rules. When paired with a four, it could also mean that an individual have already decided on a certain foundation for his/her life like getting married or getting a job that is stable for a long period of time, sometimes it could also mean that there's a certain level of stagnation or limitation because of too much power if it pertains to leadership or perhaps following the rules which can make an individual limited and not have enough freedom. Fours can suggest solidity and stability but can also promote stagnation

The Number Five Cards

Number five in tarot represents upset of the stability in number four due to chaos, conflict, imbalance, strife, and uncertainty but it can also suggest a pivotal point in creating opportunities for change and growth as a result of these trials and challenges that a person have experienced. It also relates to the Hierophant in the major arcana.

- **The Number Five and the High Hierophant**

    The High Hierophant is all about conformity, authority in the spiritual laws, conservative, and one that exhibit a traditional view. He has high regard for dogmas and doctrines, and sometimes can be likened to a religious teacher. So if the High Hierophant card is paired with a five it's like the physical realm meets the spiritual realm wherein there will be a lot of challenges physically or mentally but it will help a person grow spiritually in that sense. The ego of an individual will be challenged but it can bring forth a spiritual development. Five is sort of the tipping point wherein it aims to teach the individual a lesson and also loss of control over something or someone

The Number Six Cards

Number six in tarot represents balance, reconciliation, union, fairness, cooperation and connection. It also denotes beauty, love, collaboration, justice and relationships. The number six is related to The Lovers card in the major arcana.

- **The Number Six and the Lovers**

  The Lovers card is a positive card that denotes love and connection one has for another person. It's also a passionate and spiritually driven kind of union though sometimes it can just be a simple attraction for something or someone. It's a very optimistic card not only for the aspects of relationship but also in other areas. When pulled with the number six it can suggest about the depth of passion or connection that an individual feels for another person. It also focuses on celebration, success, and sort of equilibrium, and generally has a positive impact. The Lovers card that is paired with a six also talks about the need to make decisions or choices, sometimes it's also about moving on or some form of change in terms of perception.

The Number Seven Cards

Number seven in tarot denotes a flux in the spiritual growth of an individual and that one must deal with through reflection, assessment or gaining wisdom. The number seven is also known as a deep and spiritual number. This card challenges a person in some way to grow and develop values or identity that's aligning with the spiritual self. If you pulled a lot of sevens in a reading, it can mean that the subject should reach a philosophical solution. It is related in the Chariot card found in the major arcana.

- **The Number Seven and the Chariot**

    The Chariot card denotes success, triumph and using one's will, power and intention to achieve a goal, there's also a lot of assertiveness, vitality and taking control of life. Sevens on the other hand is a point of flux or challenges to make an individual know more about oneself. These challenges will make an individual realize his/her positive or negative virtues, values, vices and identities. When pulled with the Chariot card it can mean that there'll be a test with one's beliefs or inner strength, sometimes it can also mean that one should figure out a way to deal with the change that's happening in one's life so that a person can learn or grow. The seven cards that's paired with the Chariot in general focuses on the struggles and challenges one must overcome physically or spiritually, it will test one's belief and character and will also make a person bring out the best in them through overcoming these challenges.

The Number Eight Cards

Number eight in tarot is all about a person's personal power, movement and manifestation. One's power can be utilize to break down limitations and accomplish a dream or goal, however, effort is required to make this happen but the rewards in the end has a potential to be fulfilling; misdirected power can result to imbalances. The number eight cards relates to the Strength card in the major arcana.

- **The Number Eight and the Strength**
  The Strength card is not a complex card but it has a profound meaning if it comes up in a reading and when paired with number eight cards. It denotes an inner strength and the power of one's inner being. If your subject gets this card it could mean that a person has control over his/her own will and intention. An individual is most likely trying to achieve things actively or in a sort of conscious effort. It's also a card that is quite balance because it can mean that a person

is not necessarily struggling to achieve something but he/she recognizes that there's an inner strength that he/she can develop to make something happen. There's self – control and one can overcome any sort of impulses, this person can also be one with nature as well as the animals around. Generally The Strength card means that a person can transform any sort of negativity and turn situations into something positive because of the fact that he/she is more centered and internally strong. When paired with the number eight cards, it can relate to a person's inner power to get from where they are to where they want to be. It emphasizes on the fact that one can move out of any situation or get past some form of self - limitation to achieve something.

The Number Nine Cards

Number nine in tarot represents fruition, attainment, bringing something to conclusion and it also means that a person is already near the end. All of the minors are associated with The Hermit in the major arcana which show a solitary figure and an inner journey. It can also mean letting go of the past to prepare the upcoming transition.

- **The Number Nine and the Hermit**

The Hermit card is about the internal journey of a person, it encourages a person to withdraw from the external factors or environment to work more on one's internal world. It's also about intuition and inner guide through solitude, meditation or reflection to discover more about one's self physically, mentally and spiritually. It can also be a period of isolation but it will make a person face his/her fears and also have some form of enlightenment. The number nine card is a point where a person is almost at the end of the cycle because it's near the number ten. It's a point where one has attained a certain amount of success and he/she is on the last leg of his/her own journey. When these cards are paired, it can mean that a person has gone through some experiences already and it encourages an individual to just keep going or give it a final push because the end is almost there. It can also mean that one is being cautious because the person had gone through so much that he/she is being protective of whatever one has achieved. It's a call to maintain the discipline and attitude to carry something through the end. When the number nine cards and the Hermit are paired, it generally is all about introspection and how a person has learned so

much through the journey that he/she had been
through.

The Number Ten Cards

Number ten in tarot denotes completion, fulfillment
and the end of a cycle. It also represents renewal or a new
beginning. It also talks about transformation, change or
rebirth. It is the point of the end and the beginning. The
number ten cards relates to the Wheel of Fortune in the
major arcana which is all about the end of cycles.

- **The Number Ten and the Wheel Fortune**
  If your subject has reached the ten it simply means
  that one is at the end of a cycle, a chapter in life, a
  journey or has reached completion in terms of work
  or dreams and even in relationships. When the Wheel
  of Fortune card is paired with the ten of swords for
  example, it means that something destructive has
  been broken down and that something new is going
  to start shortly. If paired with the ten of wands, it can
  mean that a person carried a lot of responsibility
  throughout his/her journey and had gone through a
  lot of tough situations but even if that's the case, even
  if the person has really depleted himself, it can still be
  rejuvenated because he had reached the end. For ten

of pentacles, it often means that a person has been successful in terms of finances or any type of monetary endeavor as well as connection with the family; the wealth is passed down and the project has been a success. The ten of cups focuses more on the success of one's inner world and it shows balance and harmony as well as fulfillment and joy in oneself. There's optimism and expansion as well when it is paired with the Wheel of Fortune. The number ten and the Wheel of Fortune in general focus on new hope, a better future and that life is a cycle so you can always expect for change to happen either in a positive or negative way.

Chapter Six: Card Combinations, Patterns and Elemental Dignities

As a proficient reader when you have two cards that come up in a reading that have similar meaning, it's really quite subtle so it's important to make sure that your customers or subjects really understand the message that's been given to them. There are several ways that you can end up finding patterns in a reading. In this section, we'll focus on the most common examples of cards that often come up

in a reading or the cards that are often paired so that you can
see the patterns of how to read these card combinations and
hopefully derived a much stronger message out of them that
could be relevant to your subject.

Similar Meanings

The similarity of meanings and card combinations can be
adjusted or change depending on which card it is paired
with. Examples of cards that often come up and have a
relatively similar meaning are the Seven of Pentacles and the
Knight of Pentacles; the Eight of Swords and the Devil Card;
Two of Cups and Five of Cups; Ten of Swords and Wheel of
Fortune. Take note though that these cards can come with
other pairs or come up more often, it can come in various
ways but it's almost as if these cards are carrying around the
same energy with them.

The Seven of Pentacles and the Knight of Pentacles

The Seven of Pentacles have meaning associated with
attention to detail, diligence, patience, sometimes it signifies
delayed results or slow progress that could be happening in
your subject's life. It can also mean that the person has not
been really able to harvest or get results on whatever he/she
is working on, so it generally means that the person could be

working hard, putting a lot of effort and being patient in order to reap the rewards. Often times, this card is paired with Knight of Pentacles which has some sort of similar connotations, (of course if the Seven of Pentacles is paired with a different card, it will have a totally different meaning), the Knight of Pentacles or sometimes referred to as the Prince of Pentacles can often relate to stability, loyalty, being very practical, pragmatic and a card that associates with seeking security, does things slowly, someone who thinks about the kind of effort that he/she is willing to put into in order to achieve a certain growth or progress without rushing in.

So from all these meanings and associated adjectives, you can see that from the two cards, there are similarities of meanings – there's slowness, practicality, pragmatism, there's also steady of progress, and the theme of "not reaping rewards immediately unless much effort is exerted." These will be the highlights when the two cards come up, so from those similar meanings, you can easily interpret that your subject might not be reaching fulfillment, completion or success at this point of their lives, and that they may need to be patient because there will be a steady but slow progress that will be happening.

These meanings that you draw from the similar connotations of both cards can be related to your subject's career, relationship, dreams etc. which means that they might need to be patient in their work or perhaps put in a lot of effort in their relationships; it could be reliable but steady not necessarily full of passion but perhaps practicality.

Now if the Seven of Pentacles is paired with a different card, say for example, the Hanged Man, it can have a sort of similar meaning but the focus of the message will most likely be different. The Hanged Man card is associated with words like surrender, pause, reflection, inaction, and standstill. It is still related to the meaning of the Seven of Pentacles because the theme is all about something that is not coming to fruition right away but in this case it could be less on the practicality or hard work. Perhaps, the focus of the message is that the rewards will definitely be delayed due to some kind of standstill along the way.

These meanings were derived simply because that's the strongest common denominator between the two cards, so as a tarot card reader that's what you should highlight more. These are some examples where parts of them have similar meaning which is why the message becomes very strong in the reading.

The Eight of Swords and the Devil Card

These cards again have similar meanings; the Eight of
Swords is a card that is associated with self – limitation, it
often means that the subject could be restricting themselves
and not moving out of the situation even if he/she can. This
card also means that there's a lack of clarity and vision or
sort of self – entrapment because the subject may not know
where he/she is going and have no idea how to get there.

The Devil Card on the other hand is associated with
meanings like temptation, attachment to things, and
entrapment but it's more about dealing with one's 'inner
demons' or inner imprisonment. It could also mean
attaching oneself to something that is not healthy or good.
So from the meaning of these two cards, you can focus on
the part that they are binding themselves to a thought or
belief system as well as to things or people that could be
limiting your subject and not allowing them to be free.
There's an attachment issue, self – entrapment or self –
limitation.

Now, if you paired the Devil Card with the Seven of
Cups it can again have similar meaning but the focus of the
message is different. As with the Seven of Cups, it's a card
associated with imagination, visions, delusions, skewed

perspective, and moving to things that are not in your best interest. Most of the time, this card represents substance abuse if the person is in a difficult situation, so if this card is paired with the Devil Card (with a meaning of attachment to things that aren't healthy), the message you can focus on is that your subject could be attaching or depending themselves on something like a substance, toxic relationships or something that is not healthy.

Two of Cups and Five of Cups

The Two of Cups is about making connection with others and building a bond with people. The Five of Cups on the other hand is also about a person's emotional life, intuition, feelings and relationships with others, how a person reconcile things, and about the inner world. So if you encounter pulling out two or more cups in a reading that means that your subject is dealing with some kind of emotional part of themselves or relationship situations. In this case, you can interpret it as something that's been loss (probably due to a breakup or death of a loved one) and your subject may need to be positive about it. So if it's a relationship issue, it means that your subject should look at the positive side of it even if it could be something of a breakup, you could advise him/her to let go or move on.

If the Two of Cups is paired with a Three of Cups, there's still a cup theme (or a relationship theme) but it's with more than one person like friendships, family etc. It represents your communication with others or positive connection with people. So if these two cards are paired, you can interpret it in a way where there's emotional situation going on but it's on a positive level and it's more than one person. The point is you're looking for a pattern but each cup has a different meaning or has your subject is focusing on a different area at the moment.

Ten of Swords and Wheel of Fortune

The number ten usually means that you're nearing the end of the cycle or you're at the end of the cycle, so that could mean that the person has gone through a lot or have experienced a lot of things already. The number ten is the closing of a cycle, the swords represent some challenges that a person have been through. So the Ten of Swords card has come to a point where a person is in a collapse kind of situation, however, it's also saying that a new cycle is about to begin, so the person has to take a look at how you can prepare for that next cycle.

The Ten of Swords is connected to the Wheel of Fortune because the Wheel of Fortune card represents a cyclical nature of things, so that means that a person go through phases and move from one to another, there's always a change or flux and it also talks about the "seasons of life." These card combinations can mean that your subject is at the end of that particular situation or even in their life – that they're probably about to close that "chapter" but a new one is coming.

Elemental Dignities

Essentially elemental dignities will make you determine if the card is well – dignified or ill – dignified. It also depends on what other card combination is next to it. You'll learn if a card combination has an element that speaks the same language or opposite language. Elemental dignities basically pertain to the relationships of each element to one another.

Qualities of Elements

Before determining the relationship of each element, you must first know the qualities or characteristics of the elements in a card. Just like in any other field particularly subjects that deal with nature or energy fields, the elements are composed of Air, Fire, Water and Earth. In Tarot cards, the air element is represented by swords, the water element is represented by cups, the Earth element is pentacles and the fire is represented by wands. The four elements relates to the four kinds found in the tarot deck. By looking at the four elements, a reader can determine some of its characteristics.

There's also the concept of polarity in the four elements which is also divided by two; the first pair is Fire (Wands) and Air (Swords) which are also called active elements; the second pair is Water (Cups) and Earth (Pentacles) which are also called passive elements. The former paired elements are masculine and the latter pair is feminine.

Masculine elements are active, outgoing, extroverted and has a "yang energy." It can also be described as direct, assertive, sustaining, autonomous and often times self – motivated. These masculine elements also focuses on the self and its 'powers' comes from within oneself. On the other hand, the feminine elements have characteristics that are receptive, indirect, passive, introverted, soft, intuitive, nurturing and it has a tendency to look outside of oneself especially for advice or verifications.

Elemental Dignities and its Relationships

Now that you've learned what the elements are and their representation in the tarot deck, the next important thing to know is how these elements relate to one another. As a reader, you're going to encounter combinations that come up in readings so you have to know its meaning and relationships because it can also affect the message of the cards.

The fire element is usually opposite the water which makes sense because water can put out fire, so having these elements means that they weaken one another. Once these elements show up in a reading you can easily determine that those opposing energies are weakening one another and there's also a flux between these two characteristics or aspects of life that are showing up. Another elemental pairs that weaken each other is air and earth because the air is above and the earth is below.

Cards of the same element like fire (wands) and air (swords) which are also masculine strengthen each other. On the other hand, feminine elements like water (cups) and earth (pentacles) also speak the same language which therefore strengthens each other as well. Elements that neutralized each other are fire to earth as well as air to water. These things could be quite hard to remember but what you can do is to give them acronyms or have your own method of memorizing these concepts so you can easily relate it during your readings.

So basically when a card is 'elementally well dignified' that means it is being strengthened by the card next to it, on the other hand if a card is 'elementally ill dignified' it is being weakened by the card beside it. So if for example, a card shows up and it's a sword, and then it is next to another sword then it is at its strongest point because it can express its full potential and therefore elementally well dignified. If a card is in the same suit, it's going to speak the same language and vice – versa. So if you pulled a sword (air) and the card next to it is a pentacle (earth) it weakens one another and therefore it is elementally ill dignified.

Well – Dignified (Strong Position) Cards

In this section, you'll learn some examples of what it means to have a well – dignified cards. These cards have similar polarity (either masculine or feminine) elemental energy to it. We'll take a look at the Three of Wands and King of Wands; Three of Wands and King of Swords for the well – dignified cards and the Eight of Pentacles and Knight of Swords for the ill – dignified examples.

Three of Wands and King of Wands

As what you've learned, wand cards are equal to fire element and therefore has a masculine energy that is well dignified. These cards have similar characteristics; it is active, outgoing and has clarity in the decision – making process. So once these two cards are pulled, it can mean that your subject has a significant amount of masculine energy and that he/she is not going to have difficulty in terms of focus or being direct. They will pretty much force themselves to make something happen to accomplish a particular goal; they could also be assertive and self – motivated. So studying the elemental aspect of the cards can make a reader say not just the meaning of the cards or literal interpretation of it but also be able to recognize the polarity of the elements it represents. As you can see the card is well dignified and therefore is at its highest expression if you look at it this way.

Three of Wands and King of Swords

As what you've learned earlier wands are represented by fire and swords are represented by air which is another masculine energy. It may not be quite well – dignified compared to Three of Wands card and the King of Wands card (since it's basically of the same element) but it's still

well positioned because they're speaking the same language
– the more outgoing masculine language and because fire
strengthens air and vice – versa. So if the King of Swords is
paired with the Three of Wands your subject may have
created something to a certain point but at this point must
make certain logical decisions or really analyze something to
create a sound decision going forward.

Four of Cups and Four of Pentacles

Cups (water) and Pentacles (earth) are both feminine
polarity. They share characteristics that are receptive,
passive, introverted and have a tendency to look on the
outside to figure out what to do. Since they are both
feminine, they are well dignified cards and the fact that their
numbers are the same means that they also speak the same
language so it has a lot of similarities to it however, this is
where you have too much passive energy and potentially
too little progress wherein a person could feel as if they're
being controlled by other things or being in a passive
position.

The number four signifies stability but it can also
mean that there could be intrinsic limitations that prevent an
individual from growing or achieving something. If you
pulled out a bunch of feminine energy and the number four

then there's a lot of passivity or stagnation or maybe that individual is stuck in a certain position and that the only way is to take a risk to be able to get out of that restriction to be able to learn. You can also advice your subject to get in touch with a more masculine energy in order to help them to move forward or get out of their own "box." On the other hand, if you pulled out cards and saw a lot of active masculine energy it could mean that there's conflict, fight or competition, the solution is to get in touch with the female elements or passive principles.

Ill – Dignified (Weak Position) Card

The examples in this section will focus on cards that are opposite each other or weakened by the card next to it.

Eight of Pentacles and Knight of Swords

The Eight of Pentacles is an earth element and the Knight of Swords is an air element which means they are opposite and therefore weakening each other and not speaking the same language. The Knight of Swords card has a masculine polarity to it since it is an air element, it has characteristics of being action – oriented, outgoing, adventurous, flexible and pretty much has a masculine energy to it. Pentacles in general is all about manifestations in the physical realm, it has tendencies to move slower and only working on things that are tangible and kind of earth bound. When it comes to the Eight of Pentacles represent someone who diligently works, takes time to develop a skill and someone who is working very hard over a long period of time.

So if you think about it, the Eight of Pentacles is all about taking one's time to create something while the Knight of Swords focuses on direct action and just going after whatever idea comes to mind. These characteristics are opposing and doesn't go very well together, if your subject pulled this card combinations, it could mean that they are in a flux between these two opposing energies so most likely these energies are fighting against one another or perhaps your subject needs to be aware it because it's not going to help them in moving forward.

Your subject may also need some sort of compromise to these two opposing elements in order to bring things in harmony or balance. It could also mean that the Eight of Pentacles need to accept the brilliant ideas of the Knight of Swords and the Knight of Swords should need to slow down and take time to think things out. So you need to let your subject know that they have opposing energies that they need to be aware of and work out.

Chapter Seven: Card Placements within a Tarot Spread

In this section, you'll learn some of the ways in which a card is strengthened or weakened depending on the placement within a reading; it can be related to an elemental dignity or other meanings. Knowing the card placement or even card reversal within a tarot spread can affect your reading as well. I'm going to give you some examples on how card placement may have an impact on the cards meaning and how it is strengthened or weakened by being in a particular position.

Cards That Fall in an Outcome/Final/Future Position

Many different spreads have some type of outcome or final position, so if you have that kind of spread for your subject you'll know that those cards are in a very strong position because it's showing you a final outcome or a point of completion.

- **Six of Wands** - Six of Wands, six is a number that represents a certain level of completion; it's also a card that celebrates victory in a positive way.

- **Ten of Pentacles** - Ten of Pentacles is another great card in the outcome position, if you have a ten that shows up even in other types of cards, it usually signifies a final point in some type of cycle, as for Ten of Pentacles, it's a positive outcome for some kind of success in career, relationships, family or other areas. If the ten is in the Swords card or Wands it could be quite a challenging end or one that has been through strife compared to cups and pentacles. But again, seeing a ten is great because it means that the cycle is in a final point and a new cycle is coming.

- **The World** - The World card in itself is already showing an outcome or completion as well, it also means putting an effort over a period of time and seeing success on a physical level. It can also have a spiritual connotation and it's a well dignified card because it's in a very strong position.

- **The Sun** - The Sun card in a final position means a positive outlook; it also shows confidence and just a naturally strong card to have for the outcome.

- **The Ten of Cups** - Ten of Cups shows happiness, connections with loved ones, abundance and a lot of great things have happened for an individual. It also signifies an emotional satisfaction.

- **The Wheel of Fortune** - The Wheel of Fortune again shows a level of completion in phases or cycles. You can assume that one cycle is ending and another one will begin soon. This card also holds a strong position in the outcome reading.

Cards that Fall in a Challenge or Obstacle Position

Cards that are in positive positions aren't the only cards that are strengthened because what we're talking about here in this chapter is whether a card is well dignified in the sense of its meaning. The card must be in its purest meaning when it comes up, so cards that are challenging or difficult in a reading must be something that your client or subject might need to overcome.

- **Three of Swords** – is a card that shows separation, difficulty and denotes some kind of pain or anger that has been caused by difficult relationships that can be felt in a very deep level. So if this card comes up in a challenge position, it's about how your subject can overcome the pain and difficulty that he/she has experienced and how to deal with it.

- **The Devil Card** – the devil card denotes some form of attachment mentally or physically that might be holding your subject back from being whoever he/she wants to be or do.

- **Five of Cups** – this card denotes that one should overcome some sort of grief or despair that he/she sometimes feel and go through. Your subject should learn how to deal with those emotions as best as they can to move forward.

- **Nine of Swords -** this card in a challenge position denotes that one should overcome personal anxieties or difficulties. Your subject should believe in his/herself and not over - analyzed everything mentally.

Reading Cards in Tarot Spread Position

In this section, you'll learn how to read a negative card in a positive placement or vice – versa. Tarot cards in general looks at the scope of a human's life or an individual's psyche and how we live our lives. Every card in the tarot conveys some kind of lesson that you can learn from whether it's in a positive or negative position. You need to understand that nothing is black and white – which means that nothing is completely positive or negative; there are always two sides to it and a lesson to learn from.

Positive Cards in a Negative Placement vs. Negative Cards in a Positive Placement

This concept can be very hard to grasp especially if you're a beginner it's because most newbie readers read cards in its literal form or the meaning of it but if the card is placed in a contradicting situation it can be hard to analyze and draw meaning from. As with most expert tarot card readers, they have developed their own reading system in reading cards that are either in a negative or positive placement but their common denominator or perhaps the guiding principle is that tarot cards are not one dimensional, even if it's a positive cards there'll still be some negative aspect to it, same with negative cards. Some readers refer to it as a shadow, warning or edge if a card has positive meaning but is placed in a negative position or vice – versa. If you understand the edge or shadows of a card, you'll be able to understand how to read them in any kind of placement. Here are some examples:

- **The Sun Card**

The Sun card is a positive card so if it lands in an outcome or final position within a spread then you can automatically say that it will be about optimism, happiness, fulfillment or a person has shine in its own way in life because that's the usual denotation of that card. Now, if the Sun Card comes up in a negative position, it may denote that your subject may not be living life to the fullest, they may not be acknowledging the joys in their life, your client may not be fully expressing who they are or who they want to be or what if your client does not feel free to express something or may not have the freedom to live life on their own terms.

Those are the ideas that you could ask or share to your client if a positive card like this comes up in a negative position.

- **Three of Swords**

The Three of Swords card is a difficult card or a negative card because it usually denotes pain, separation, betrayal, isolation, heartbreak and suffering. So if this card comes up in a positive placement, the edge or shadow of this card could be a call for healing. The lesson or the message you can convey to your client is to determine how one can start the healing process or identify and acknowledge those sufferings so that they'll be able to start healing in that particular area of their life. If your client is asking for an advice and this card comes up, then you can tell him/her to face the pain they are feeling and possibly do something with what could help them heal a particular feeling or angst they may have.

- **The Emperor Card**

The Emperor card is all about structure, order, formation so it can be related to rules and regulations. It also has some kind of authority or leadership quality to it. It's a positive card that could be great if pulled in an outcome position because it can mean that one is becoming a leader or perhaps one needs to pay attention to a structure to maintain an orderly kind of environment. But if this card is in a negative position, it can mean that the power or control brought about by leadership can be too much to handle. It can mean that an individual is over -powering or over - controlling a situation; there's probably too much rules, laws or regulations that can be a hindrance to freedom or creativity; it can also mean that a person is too limited in his/her approach and he/she may need to let go of some of these limiting beliefs. So if this card is in a negative placement, it will focus on how much control or power is happening as well as the how the structure may limit freedom to a person or to other people.

- **Nine of Swords**

  The Nine of Swords is a negative card that's all about anxiety, mental anguish, depression and some sort of feedback loop where a person is constantly thinking about something that's painful or obsessing about something that is bothering him/her for a long time. It could also bring up a level of being ill due to a stressful situation. There's a lot of strife and isolation for this card but if the Nine of Swords come up in a positive position, the advice you can give to your subject to overcome a situation is to maybe be able to step back and figure out what it is that's causing them these anxieties so they can find a way to solve it, kind of getting to the root cause of the problem. Another meaning you can derive from this card in a positive way is again healing, so perhaps this card is telling your subject to take time to heal and just let it all out, let all the tears flow so that he/she can be cleanse inside out and be able to let go of all the things that is troubling them and move past this difficulty.

- **Nine of Cups**

The Nine of Cups denotes that one hasn't reached the end yet but they're almost there. It's a positive card that represent ones emotional self or inner world, relationship with oneself or with others, creativity and the likes (remember it's a feminine polarity). It also means that a person has reached a certain level of abundance or fulfillment but they are alone. So the edge of this card if it's placed in a negative position is that the person is "alone," meaning that the individual may not be connecting or sharing what they have accomplish with other people. You can also consider a level of complacency as well as overindulgence in the individual's part.

- **The Five of Cups**

The Five of Cups has an intrinsic edge to it; as you now know, the cups talks all about relationships, emotions, inner world, creativity and intuition. This card in particular denotes loss, grief, emotional pain, and difficulty to let go so this is in itself a negative card. So the edge of the card when it is placed in a positive position is that there's some kind of hope after all this pain and strife, and it means that an individual needs to let go of whatever he/she loss in order to move on to see the positive things that are still there.

Three Card Spreads

Three card spreads are usually used to see what's coming up for the next three months or possibly the kind of events that will unfold with regards to the subject's physical, mental or even emotional aspect. What you can do is to let your client choose one card for each of the next three months for them to have a glimpse of the future. If you're doing to a three card spread what you can do is to assign the first card that is picked for the next month (not the month you are in), and then the next card is for the consecutive month and so on. In this section, we'll give you some examples on how to read cards that could mean the next three months for your subject.

Example #1: The Four of Cups, Ace of Wands, Four of Wands

This is where the other lessons will come in, so if you remember the principle of elemental dignities from previous chapters you can use that in initially reading the cards and incorporate other tarot reading principles from there.

From this set of example, you'll notice that Wands card are predominant since there are two out of three. Predominance of wands or the fire element energy is going to be important for the next three months. It could mean that an individual may develop some type of interest or passion in some endeavor or a certain drive and energy. They might also use a more masculine polarity which means that they'll probably be more action – oriented in order to achieve something. They'll also probably start off the next three months with the cup energy which means that there could be an emotional element involve.

You can also take a look at another aspect which is the numbers of the cards. So from this example, there's a four of cups and four of wands, as you've previously learned in the numbers chapter, the number four signifies structure, order, stability, limitation and there's possibly a manifestation in the physical world. So you can look at it in a way of the flow of events, will there be stagnation in the next three months or what kind of progress is going to happen, is it from stagnation to action or vice – versa etc. So from this example, the four of cups (the first month) denotes stagnation, the ace of wands denotes not much action; the four of wands denotes a significant form of action, so that could be the possible flow in the next three months.

The advice you can give to your client is that in the first month (four of cups) they may want to determine what's stopping them from doing something or focus on the possible opportunities around them. You can also suggest feeling their emotions about certain things but not get stuck with it and recognize that the difficulty they are feeling at the moment is temporary.

For the next month, the ace of wands suggests that you have to figure out how to maximize that opportunity because you'll experience a spark of inspiration, passion, enthusiasm or an idea, you'll have the energy in doing something not just in career related things but other aspects as well. So this is the month to actually start doing something and taking that first step towards a particular interest.

The third card (four of wands) suggests that by the third month, your subject may have already manifest something from that spark of interest, it also suggests that an individual has prosper from it or made it stable, in short there'll be some type of success involve or a positive outcome in career, relationship or other aspects.

Example #2: The World, Four of Cups, Six of Wands

Again, you'll have to look at the flow of the cards, so you can check out if there are similarities or none at all, the numbers, the cards and the overall flow. If there's no repeating aspect to the cards just like this example it doesn't necessarily mean that there's no pattern – it's just not that obvious. So you have to go back to finding the flow of events for the cards and what they could possibly mean.

For this set, the example will be a query about relationships. The first card pulled for the first month is The World card, the second is the Four of Cups, and the third is the Six of Wands – so if you think about it the pattern is like an up and down sort of thing which can apply to the status of your subject's relationship in the next three months. The relationship starts at the top (The World Card), then it goes downhill (Four of Cups) and climbs up again (Six of Wands). So overall, you can assume that there were aspects of the relationship that's fulfilling as represented by the world card and maybe that relationship became grounded or serious, then at some point they could experience some sort of challenge that pertains to emotions which is represented by the four of cups, your subject may be undergoing some sort of unhappiness in a particular aspect of their relationship and they may need to figure out what's really going on or perhaps what's causing that feeling of discontentment in order to overcome that downhill flow.

The six of wands represent some success, triumph, and optimism since the number six also means a sense of balance and harmony. It can mean that the relationship has overcome whatever emotional challenge or difficulty that they have experience.

Example #3: Situation Cards, Obstacle Cards, Outcome Cards

In this example, we'll use The Hanged Man, The Lovers, and The Chariot. Now, these cards are all in the Major Arcana so it means that a situation is of major importance or significant for the individual's spiritual or psychological level. It's not about the physical surroundings or daily life (minor arcana), it's going to represent something that is much profound than that.

- **Situation Card: The Hanged Man**
  The Hanged Man is all about the spiritual state or the unconscious state. This card is not about dealing with daily life, it's more of connecting to oneself or in a

spiritual level. So if you pulled this card for a situation placement, it can mean that an individual is contemplating, it can also mean a difficult time because the person is not necessarily moving forward or the situation is at a standstill or suspension. This card suggests a period of reflection or that a person should look at things from a different perspective. Your subject may also spiritually need to connect but he/she is not connecting to a certain thing.

- **Challenge Card: The Lovers**

  The Lovers card is associated with passion or spiritually love, where a person connects with someone or something that has great depth or spiritual meaning. So if you pulled this card for a challenge placement, it can mean that it's related to choices that one needs to make or the crossroads that a person is currently on. The obstacle that is represented by this card is that a person may be lacking clarity or that one must make decisions in order to move forward.

- **Outcome Card: The Chariot**

  The Chariot card is associated with success, triumph or having control over a situation in order to take oneself to a certain place or goal. This card represents decision making and also pertains to the freedom to use one's will or power to do certain tasks.

So the flow for this set of cards is that an individual is moving from a lack of clarity and not knowing which way to go as represented by the Hanged Man, then making decisions (The Lovers) and finally having that internal will and drive to put something into play to make a progression and move forward as represented by The Chariot card.

Chapter Eight: Card Reversals and Timing

There are various theories about how readers can interpret the meaning of a reversed card, in this section though we'll only brush up on some common meanings of reversed cards. If your client is asking what he/she needs to learn or the challenge that needs to be overcome the reversed cards are in a very strong position because it can show the avenue that your subject can address or change. The timing in tarot cards deals with how your subject should approach a situation or the kind of timing is on the current reading. The timing will show you how something are going to unfold or what your subject needs to know in terms of going to the next step.

Card Reversals

We'll provide some examples of how you can interpret a meaning of the card when it is drawn or pulled out in a reverse position. Basically, you just have to sort of reverse its meaning or put it in another perspective.

- **Eight of Swords** – this card generally means that someone is bound by a circumstance or perception and that a person needs to recognize that they can overcome that, so if this card is reversed, it can signify that an individual is breaking through some of the constraints that are imposed upon a person or perhaps oneself. It can also mean freeing oneself from some kind of limiting factors.

- **The Devil Card** – as mentioned previously, it can mean attachment from certain things that aren't healthy or at a person's best interest. So if it's reverse, it can mean that an individual is in a more growing awareness or in a state where an individual wants to be free of a particular attachment.

- **Eight of Wands** – if this card is reverse, it can have issues in terms of moving forward because there could be some issues, delays or even difficulties.

- **Six of Swords** – once this card is reverse it could also mean that there'll be delays in moving through a certain situation or leaving the past behind either physically or mentally.

Timing in Tarot Cards

Sometimes in a reading you may have to deal with what kind of approach your client should do. If you have a reading where your subjects or clients are asking an advice on a particular situation they are in, the following examples will show you how to recognize some cards in the tarot deck.

Seven of Pentacles and Knight of Pentacles

Seven of Pentacles is all about having diligence and patience to work hard on something but not being able to reap the rewards right away. So it's a card that will tell you and your subject that something in their life may not be coming into fruition at the moment or any time soon. Knight of Pentacles similarly is a card that denotes stagnation. The Knight of Pentacles does things slowly and is quite methodical compared to the Knight of Swords or Knight of Wands; he will not rush into doing things but if he decides to do things he will do it well and will take his time in doing it.

If these kinds of cards come up, the timing will be slower, probably more methodical, it's something that's going to happen over a period of time and your client may not necessarily see the rewards of whatever he/she is doing right away, and patience may be required.

The Hanged Man and Four of Swords

Both of these cards denote that quick action and activity is not going to happen. The Hanged Man card can mean that your subject may need to pause or reflect. It can also mean that your subject may not have the energy to do a particular endeavor at this time. It can also mean not being able to move forward and that an individual may need to surrender something to move forward. The Four of Swords is about a period of recuperation and it mainly denotes a healing phase probably from a stress or a broken relationship. So these cards can tell your subject that things may not be moving forward at this time in terms of unfolding events.

The Knight of Swords and Eight of Wands

The Eight of Wands is a card that is looking forward to something; it has some positive element to it and usually denotes a fast pace of progress or being able to move forward. It has a lot of quick energy in it and some information can also come to you which will help you accomplish things faster. Knight of Swords is a similarly active card, so if your client asks you how something is going to unfold or the timing of a certain event, once you pull these cards it can mean that something is going to happen very quickly but of course, there's also some precaution because you might need to also take a step back and not rush too much.

Cards Denoting Transition or New Beginnings

Cards that show transition or change can also be found in the Major Arcana and the minor ones, in this section, you'll learn some of these cards and how they suggest change or new beginnings in an individual's life.

- **The Death Card** – this card notoriously means that an individual is going through some kind of change and because of that transition; the person will be changed, moved through it and possibly come out a different person either growing or developing in some way.

- **The Tower of Card** – it denotes an abrupt change and may mean that an individual may sometimes need to let go of whatever we are holding to allow a significant change to occur.

- **The Fool Card** – denotes that an individual may need to take a leap of faith, start something fresh or doing something that you haven't done before is required.

- **Six of Swords** – denotes that you need to move through a situation because a better one is ahead. It can also mean that an individual may need to move to a new location or travel for a change.

For transition cards, your subject may need to recognize that a new start, a new learning or a new approach is required, these things are important in readings that has a position around that particular theme.

Relationship Cards

If you're going to do a reading on relationships, there are a lot of cards in the tarot deck that speak clearly about relationships. Regardless if a card has a positive connotation or it shows a negative spin or some sort of difficulty as long as it's in the realm of relationships, these cards will have a strong position in a reading.

- **Seven of Cups** – this card in terms of relationship suggests that there are lots of emotions or desire but an individual may have lots of choices and might not be clear of how they feel or who to choose. It also denotes not having clarity in a relationship.

- **Knight of Cups** – this card can mean the style of a particular relationship and tends to be in a romantic placement.

- **Ten of Cups** – it denotes positivity, a sense of completion and happiness in a certain relationship.

- **The Knight of Pentacles** – it is a very practical earth card that denotes an individual has worked very hard, and in terms of relationship one or both parties are independent and self – sufficient. One or both parties may not want the kind of relationship that is being too dependent of one another.

- **Five of Swords** – the number five is denoting strife which can signify difficulties in a relationship. It can also mean a lot of competition or struggle.

Chapter Nine: Reading a Tarot Card for the Day

The notion of pulling a card every day works best if you really take the time to 'feel' your cards or sit with your tarot deck for at least a couple of minutes every morning so you can sort of feel the energy within these cards. The idea behind this is to focus or become aware of the kind of energy you have for that particular day. It's not necessarily about programming your day or having a planned activity but it's more of having that sense of both the positive and negative aspects because it can also affect how the cards will show up. This chapter will also cover how to interpret meaning that's "not" in a reading or patterns that aren't obvious.

How to Read a Tarot Card for the Day

For you to be able to interpret a card you pulled for a particular day, you have to pay attention to the different sides of the card and observe the energy you feel for yourself or with other people. Say for example you pulled out a King of Cups card, you can first lay out its literal meaning like this card is someone who is a nurturer, who cares deeply and can be strongly attached to things or people they have a relationship with. Another kind of meaning you could be getting from this card could also pertain to someone who is protective or quite controlling; there could also be abundance of emotion in general.

You can relate the meanings or characteristics of the card in your experiences throughout the day. Of course, not everyone has the luxury to recap their whole day or record every significant thing that happen (if any) but you have to be aware of things like the energy or characteristics of the card and how it played out its different attributes during the day. You can learn from that so you can have a better understanding of how you can use it in the future whenever you're doing a card reading for the day.

So, basically there's no formula or standard method even for expert tarot readers when it comes to interpreting a card for the day, some books or guides may tell you tips or guiding principles but it's clearly up to you on how you interpret things and relate the energies or events that happened to you with the card you pulled for that particular day, sometimes you just have to be consciously aware of it or maybe do some mental notes. The context doesn't really matter, and according to most tarot readers, the symbols of tarot cards are all parts of our lives' constellations – the more you can define and depict events in your day to day life, the more you'll be able to understand and recognize the energy from a tarot card.

What's Not in the Tarot Reading

When you're doing a reading, one of the first things you should do is to scan the cards and see if the majority of cards are in the major arcana or minor arcana. Below are some examples of situation that is not in a tarot reading and what it could mean to the interpretation or impact of the message:

Example #1: Major and Minor Arcana (Questions about Spiritual Aspect)

If the cards predominantly belong to the major arcana in a spread, the message is most likely related to a spiritual path of an individual or some kind of growth in an individual's soul. It can also mean an internal process or change in a psychological or spiritual level.

- **What's Not in the Reading: The Minor Arcana**

    Minor arcana are composed of tarot cards that are relating to everyday life or relating to situations with people as well as how an individual is processing the daily life and the struggles that come along with it. Since the sample spread doesn't have any minor arcana, it simply means that the message is not about your subject's processing in their daily life's circumstances. You can assume that the focus is about the inner growth or mental and spiritual development or connection (if the question is about relationships). Simply put, if there are no minor arcana in your spread, the message is centered on a much deeper or profound level that can affect one's soul or mental growth as well as conscience.

Example #2: Cups Card and Pentacles Card (Questions about Relationships)

One of the most common examples is when your subject asks you questions about relationships. Often times they would like to know the current status of their romantic relationship, and usually the key indicator in the realm of relationship is a Water (cups) card because it deals with the emotional element or feelings that one has for another individual. Now, what if a client asks about relationship stuff and they have pulled no cups or water cards? As an example, we'll use the pentacles card.

- **What's Not in the Reading: The Cups Card**

  When there's no cups card in a reading, it doesn't necessarily mean that there's no emotional bond or connection but perhaps the connection for a certain individual is channeled in something that is important or it's in a different focus of the relationship that's not about sharing emotion. Say for example, your subject pulled pentacles card in a reading, it could mean that the relationship at the given time is centered on grounding areas that are not emotional – it focuses perhaps on a more tangible aspect that the relationship has created like the possessions you bought together or it can also mean that they have a more practical or reliable relationship. Since pentacles card has an earth (ground bound) element to it, the relationship can also mean that it's sort of a work in progress for both individuals involve.

Example #3: Water Cards (Questions about Career)

If your client asks you about career related topics, the suits or cards relating to work are usually pentacles (how to manifest it in the physical realm) as well as wands (because it relates to one's drive or passion that one needs to accomplish a goal). So typically the cards you're looking for is a Pentacles or Wands card but what if your client didn't pulled any of that and instead pulled out cards like our examples.

So say for example, your subject pulled out nothing but water cards, you can immediately assume that there's something going on about this individual in an emotional level or they're working through something with a purpose. You can also consider their feelings like if your subject probably feels working in a project that may have an impact on their spiritual or emotional aspect or that particular project may relate to helping others and/or involves creativity.

You also have to think about if there's any emotional basis or drive to feel fulfillment on a particular goal or if your subject may need to adjust their path to fulfill something or monetize something. It may also involve a creative aspect, so you need to think about if your subject is infusing creativity in their work or perhaps they wanted to express more creativity in what they do but may not be able to have that freedom in their current jobs – so you can suggest that they could change jobs to find a more fulfilling career or something like that.

- **What's Not in the Reading: The Pentacles and Wands Card**

  If you or your subject didn't pulled any pentacles and/or wands card, as a reader you have to automatically say to your subject that he/she is focusing on other things or have been dealing with other things not related to work. Perhaps there's some kind of way that they're channeling their career goal through themselves or utilizing themselves that may not be related to a tangible work.

Example #4: Sword Cards (Questions about Career)

Here's another example regarding questions about career. If no pentacle or wand cards showed up and there's only Sword (air) cards on the spread it can mean the following:

- The individual could have a potentially good idea or has a spark of inspiration

- There's some level of truth or information and the person wants to manifest it but haven't't' done yet
- There's a chance that they might have lots of ideas but it only stays in their mental sphere and may not have been manifested into tangible results yet
- Since there are no wands in the spread, they may not know how to move a particular thought or idea forward

So if you see a lot of swords in terms of career and there are no pentacles or wands, basically it only tells you that your subject may have an idea that he/she wants to do but can't for some reason. You can advise him/her to maybe just give it a try so the idea can hopefully become real or manifest in the physical world.

Example #5: Masculine and Feminine Cards

As mentioned in previous chapters, there are two polarities – masculine and feminine. Feminine cards (Water/Cups and Earth/Pentacles) have characteristics of being more receptive, introverted, security, stability, don't want to take any risks, and it deals with a more internal world. Masculine cards (Fire/Wands and Air/Swords) on the other hand are more extroverted cards, active, and more action – oriented.

- **What's Not in the Reading: Feminine Cards**

  If for example, the question is about relationships and you only see masculine cards, you can assume that the emotional or security aspect is not the focus of the message. It can rather have an outgoing aspect to it if you pulled either a sword card or wand card; the relationship could be more direct and perhaps aims to move forward or quickly.

Chapter Ten: Putting It All Together

In this chapter, you'll learn some more techniques on how to prepare yourself and also your cards before making a reading. It's very important that you are prepared not just mentally but also intuitively. All the tips, methods and techniques given in this book will only serve as your literal guide in interpreting the tarot cards but your intuition will ultimately become your "inner guide" to help you learn the true message of the cards that will help improve your clients' lives.

Using Narratives or Storytelling in Tarot Reading

Storytelling using tarot cards could be used as a tool for your imagination to tell a story that can enhance your reading skills and make you more familiar with the energies of your card. It's not about interpreting the literal meaning of the cards, it's more about using the images and symbols of the card and how a story may evolve or unfold once it is drawn. You can pull out three cards to represent the beginning of the story, another three for the middle of the story and three more cards for the conclusion of the story. You can use narratives in tarot reading to practice self – awareness and also be more familiar with your deck; it will also help you as a reader to allow the imagery of the cards to 'talk' to you. It's not about interpretation or discernment; it focuses more on your creative imagination process.

Take the time to work with the cards you draw and then try to determine what kind of story emerges from those cards. Reflect on it and also try to notice if the story is something that is similarly related to what's going on in your life.

As an example, you must set the scene, set the tone, and probably make up some characters for your first three cards since this will serve as the introduction of your story. Then the next set of three cards will serve as the climax of your story – so there's a dilemma or some kind of action to the story. Once you have move through the introduction and the climax, you can begin to formulate a narrative out of it and just let your mind flow without thinking about the meanings of each card, just focus on the image and draw a story from there. The last set of three cards will play out as the final outcome or ending of your narrative.

Narratives or practicing storytelling with your cards tells you as a reader that there's more to tarot card reading, it's not just about answering a query or about getting direct answers or guidance from it. It's a technique to help you broaden your imagination, use your creativity and basically learn more about yourself because that will help you become a much better and effective tarot reader.

Shuffling Your Cards

"To shuffle or not to shuffle?" This is the question most asked by beginners, and it's actually interesting because this is a 'big deal' when it comes to tarot reading since shuffling of cards is a process that happens before a reading, that's why many people are asking if there's actually a significance or if there's an impact to the reading if the cards are shuffled or not. It's sort of a way to prepare your cards for a tarot reading.

There's a lot of ways in which a tarot reader can do a reading and the shuffling or not shuffling of cards depends on what kind of reading is going to be implemented, the kinds of questions that will be asked by the client or the kind of method that will be used by the reader. The notion of how a reader should shuffle a card is related to the kind of layout or spread that you're going to use for a particular reading.

Some experts will tell you to sort of 'cleanse the card' by surrounding it with crystals or some kind of energy stones to clear out the energies from its previous reading so the cards can start anew, this is not required but it depends on you if you believe in that kind of philosophy. Another method you can use if you're doing a relatively simple questioning session or simple methods of layout is to just randomly 'shuffle' the cards on the table, make a pile while these cards are faced down and then let your client draw the card because it makes the subject responsible for the card they get.

Now if you're going to do a Celtic – Cross layout for the cards wherein you have to layout 10 cards and the positions as well as the connections of the cards matter, you can organize your deck by arranging the major arcana cards (0 – 21), followed by the minor cards (ace cards to King) with wands coming first, followed by cups, swords and last is pentacles. This kind of arrangement is only a suggestion; of course you can arrange your deck in which you see fit but that order is based on how the energies come down in the tree of life. Again, it's totally up to you, if you feel that the deck must be arrange in this way or that way for a particular reading or whatnot then it's your call. What's important is you arrange them in a certain way and not just randomly shuffle them since the Celtic – Cross layout is quite a complicated method of reading tarot.

For some readers, they let their clients shuffle and cut the cards in the most comfortable way possible, not like how dealers shuffle cards in the casino sort of thing (although it can be done too) but in a way where they will feel the cards in an intuitive level before stacking them up. Again, there is no exact method of shuffling or preparing your cards; these are merely guidelines of how to do it based from various tarot readers' experiences, at the end of the day it's up to you in finding your own style of doing things.

A Step-By-Step Guide in Basic Tarot Reading

The following guidelines will get you started on how to perform a tarot reading, if you're just a beginner it's probably best if you follow the basic step provided in this section so that you can get used to the process of how to do a tarot reading. This guide applies to readings that are based on a written/oral question.

Prepare the following:

- The written/oral questions from your clients/subjects/seekers
- Your Tarot Deck (remember the tips from the previous section about how to 'cleanse the card')
- The spread or layout you will use (depends on the area that your subject/client want to focus on)
- Yourself (you must make sure that you know the basics of tarot reading and be mentally and emotionally prepared as well)

Step #1: Set the mood - do a tarot reading where you feel comfortable in and as much as possible avoid places with distractions.

Step #2: Relax your mind and your client – if it helps you can talk to your subject about his/her current feelings, if he/she is comfortable or just simply try to connect with him/her.

Step #3: Ask or Read the Question – remember though that when it comes to questions, it should not be like a yes/no type of query, it should be more about what to do in a certain situation/the best advice. Tarot readings will help a person deal with particular things not necessarily answer a direct question.

Step #4: Shuffle the cards – shuffle the cards or let your subject shuffle it

Step #5: Cut and pile the cards - you can also let your subject cut the cards until you think or feel that it's enough, then pile it up or stack it up in a manner you see fit.

Step #6: Layout the cards – you can make your subject pick out the card (depending on the type of layout you will use) and let him/her feel the energy within those cards. Once the cards are drawn, you can now place it in the appropriate position in a spread, make sure that the cards are still faced down.

Step #7: Reveal the cards – depending on the type of spread or your reading method, you can reveal each card one by one or simultaneously for you to see a connection.

Step #8: Interpret the Card – note the interpretation of each card as well as the pattern or position in which a card is placed and start analyzing or relating it to your subject's question/life. Consider the techniques mentioned in this book about the relationships of the card as well as the card placements.

Step #9: Create the story – once you have analyze or interpret the card and have considered all the other factors, you can now create a story based on the theme of the session or the query being asked

Step #10: Finish it Up – once you have interpret the cards and perhaps send the message to your clients as well as clarify their follow – up questions. You can then conclude the session and clear the deck. You can also express gratitude to your inner guide as well as your tarot cards and pack it up on its container.

Photo Credits

Page 1 Photo by user Glegle via Pixabay.com, https://pixabay.com/en/oracle-cards-tarot-card-cards-tarot-437688/

Page 2 Photo by user Kelly Hunter via Flickr.com, https://www.flickr.com/photos/inspirekelly/6146846684/

Page 37 Photo by user Rirriz via Pixabay.com, https://pixabay.com/en/tarot-cards-fortune-symbol-mystery-2414239/

Page 38 Photo retrieved from "6 Most Common Tarot Spreads and their Uses" blog via TarotProphet.com, http://tarotprophet.com/6-most-common-tarot-spreads-and-their-uses/

Page 40 Photo retrieved from "6 Most Common Tarot Spreads and their Uses" blog via TarotProphet.com, http://tarotprophet.com/6-most-common-tarot-spreads-and-their-uses/

Page 42 Photo retrieved from "6 Most Common Tarot Spreads and their Uses" blog via TarotProphet.com, http://tarotprophet.com/6-most-common-tarot-spreads-and-their-uses/

Page 45 Photo by user GerDukes via Pixabay.com, https://pixabay.com/en/tarot-cards-card-prophecy-dark-2114403/

Page 52 Photo by user valentin_mtnezc via Pixabay.com, https://pixabay.com/en/fortune-telling-tarot-letters-2458920/

Page 65 Photo by user Keith Rowley via Flickr.com, https://www.flickr.com/photos/yugen/8596190468/

Page 81 Photo by user meeralee via Flickr.com, https://www.flickr.com/photos/goddessparkle/196587067/

Page 98 Photo by user MiraDeShazer via Pixabay.com, https://pixabay.com/en/tarot-cards-magic-fortune-telling-991041/

Page 107 Photo by user tarotize via Pixabay.com, https://pixabay.com/en/tarot-crystals-pendulum-occult-1775322/

Page 116 Photo by user Bob Mical via Flickr.com, https://www.flickr.com/photos/small_realm/14225385617/

References

"6 Most Common Tarot Spreads and Their Uses"
TarotProphet.com

http://tarotprophet.com/6-most-common-tarot-spreads-and-
their-uses/

"7 Tarot Tips for Learning Tarot Card Meanings" Daily –
Tarot – Girl.com

https://www.daily-tarot-girl.com/learn-tarot/7-tarot-tips-learning-
tarot-card-meanings/

"Basic Tarot for Beginners" LovetoKnow.com

http://horoscopes.lovetoknow.com/Basic_Tarot_for_Beginne
rs

"Court Card Tarot Card Meanings" Aeclectic.net

http://www.aeclectic.net/tarot/learn/meanings/court-cards.shtml

"Guide To Tarot Cards" 7thSensePsychics.com

https://www.7thsensepsychics.com/tarot-book/tarotbook.pdf

"How Do I Commit The Tarot Card Meanings To Memory?" Biddytarot.com

https://www.biddytarot.com/how-to-commit-tarot-card-meanings-to-memory/

"How to Do A Basic Tarot Reading For Yourself Or A Friend" Mindbodygreen.com

https://www.mindbodygreen.com/0-18172/how-to-do-a-basic-tarot-reading-for-yourself-or-a-friend.html

"How to Read Tarot Cards: A Step by Step Guide" Daily-tarot-girl.com

https://www.daily-tarot-girl.com/learn-tarot/how-to-read-tarot-cards-a-step-by-step-guide/

"Learn the secrets of tarot reading: How to Memorise tarot cards" KellyStarSigns.com

http://www.kellystarsigns.com/2012/04/the-secrets-of-tarot-reading-how-to-memorise-tarot-cards/

"Learning the Tarot in 19 Lessons" PaganFederation.org
http://il.paganfederation.org/files/2013/03/LearningtheTarotin19lessons.pdf

"Major vs. Minor Arcana Tarot Cards: What's the Difference?"
Freetarotcardreadingsonline.com

http://www.freetarotcardreadingsonline.com/major-vs-minor-arcana-tarot-cards-whats-the-difference/

"Tarot 101: The Basics" Tarot.com

https://www.tarot.com/articles/tarot/about-tarot

"The Major Arcana Tarot Cards" Tarot.com

https://www.tarot.com/tarot/cards/major-arcana

"The Minor Arcana Tarot Cards" Tarot.com

https://www.tarot.com/tarot/cards/minor-arcana

"Understanding the Court Cards" TaroticallySpeaking.com

http://www.taroticallyspeaking.com/knowledge/understanding-the-court-cards/

Feeding Baby
Cynthia Cherry
978-1941070000

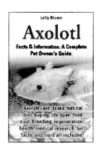

Axolotl
Lolly Brown
978-0989658430

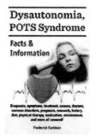

Dysautonomia, POTS
Syndrome
Frederick Earlstein
978-0989658485

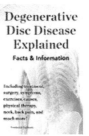

Degenerative Disc
Disease Explained
Frederick Earlstein
978-0989658485

Sinusitis, Hay Fever,
Allergic Rhinitis Explained
Frederick Earlstein
978-1941070024

Wicca
Riley Star
978-1941070130

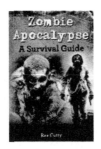

Zombie Apocalypse
Rex Cutty
978-1941070154

Capybara
Lolly Brown
978-1941070062

Eels
As Pets
A Complete Guide
Where to buy, species,
aquarium, supplies, diet, care,
tank setup, and more!

Eels As Pets
Lolly Brown
978-1941070167

Scabies and
Lice Explained
Causes, Prevention, Treatment,
and Remedies All Covered!

Information including symptoms, care,
removal, eggs, home remedies, in pets,
natural treatment, life cycle, infestation,
cure specific, and much more.

Scabies and Lice Explained
Frederick Earlstein
978-1941070017

Saltwater
Fish as Pets
A Complete Pet Owner's Guide

Saltwater Fish As Pets
Lolly Brown
978-0989658461

Torticollis
Explained
A Complete Care Guide

Causes,
Symptoms,
and Treatment
all covered!

Torticollis Explained
Frederick Earlstein
978-1941070055

Kennel Cough
Lolly Brown
978-0989658409

Physiotherapist, Physical
Therapist
Christopher Wright
978-0989658492

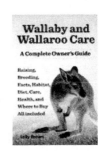

Rats, Mice, and Dormice
As Pets
Lolly Brown
978-1941070079

Wallaby and Wallaroo Care
Lolly Brown
978-1941070031

Bodybuilding Supplements
Explained
Jon Shelton
978-1941070239

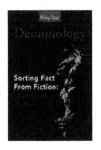

Demonology
Riley Star
978-19401070314

Pigeon Racing
Lolly Brown
978-1941070307

Dwarf Hamster
Lolly Brown
978-1941070390

Cryptozoology
Rex Cutty
978-1941070406

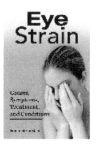

Eye Strain
Frederick Earlstein
978-1941070369

Inez The Miniature Elephant
Asher Ray
978-1941070353

Vampire Apocalypse
Rex Cutty
978-1941070321

Made in the USA
Middletown, DE
02 February 2023

23783347R00080